Wildlife of South Africa

Introduction - Over the past 200 years, much of South Africa's game has been decimated for trophies, meat, skins, horns and tusks, and the land on which they relied has been altered to make space for settlements, livestock and industry. The era of unlimited open spaces and natural game areas is past, but thanks to a few far-sighted individuals who set aside areas for conservation, and the countless people who have dedicated their lives to protecting the wildlife of their continent, most of our fauna and flora have been protected from extinction. Over the past few decades a new set of conservationists has emerged who see the land and its wildlife as South Africa's future, and who are converting huge areas of land back into wildlife areas for ecotourism. Partnerships are being made between local inhabitants and investors, so that the communities living with the wildlife benefit too, providing them with the incentive to conserve it. As a result, we are beginning to reclaim more and more land for our wildlife, with increasingly diverse opportunities to view the animals in their natural habitat.

With such a variety of landscape, extremes of climate, and the huge diversity of our vegetation, South Africa's wildlife is exceptionally diverse. With 338 mammal species co-inhabiting the varied landscape with over 900 species of bird, a diverse population of reptiles and amphibians and an innumerable number of insects, there is always something new to discover. The key to appreciating it is to spend time not only watching, but also interpreting what you see. It is our hope that the text and pictures in this book will enhance your experience in this way.

'King of the beasts' – largest African predator

Male mass: 190kg
Total length: 260cm
Shoulder height: 120cm
Female mass: 126kg
Total length: 220cm
Shoulder height: 110cm
Young: 1 - 6
Gestation: 14 - 15 weeks
Longevity: 12 - 15 years

Lion

Panthera leo

Lion - The lion is the largest African predator, and savagely rules the African night as 'The King of the beasts'. It is the only sociable cat, living in prides with a constant number of adult females, determined largely by minimum prey availability. Prides range in size from two to eighteen lionesses and their offspring, who are accompanied by one to four territorial males. The tawny lionesses form the nucleus of the pride, while adult males are immigrants that gain custody of a pride range in competition with other males.

When males take over a pride they kill cubs so that females come into oestrus. The result is that for every cub that survives to the yearling stage, lions copulate an estimated 3 000 times. The protective resident males with their showy manes regularly patrol and spray bushes in the territory, and can be heard roaring in chorus up to 10km away. Being larger than the females, the males are more conspicuous, which reduces their hunting ability. As a result, males often tackle larger, slower prey such as buffalo, or scavenge off the kills made by the lionesses.

The size and unreserved nature of the lioness makes her specifically adapted to prey on medium and large prey such as zebra and wildebeest, although the lioness is opportunistic and will attack anything from the size of a scrub hare to an adult bull giraffe weighing as much as 1 000kg! Hunting is dangerous though, and inexperienced lions are often gored by buffalo or sable antelope or kicked by zebra stallions or giraffe.

Lionesses leave the pride to give birth to litters of one to six cubs, but return to the pride to rear cubs communally

Elephant cows live in close-knit family groups

The ears form an important cooling mechanism

The youngest offspring plays with an older sibling

Mature elephant bulls roam widely, locating herds from several kilometres away through infrasound communication

Elephant - Elephants have a number of outstanding and remarkable features which separate them [fro]m all other mammals. The trunk is a prolonged nose used for smelling, for spraying water over the [elep]hant's body when it is bathing or dust when it is dust-bathing, and for carrying food and water to [its] mouth in order to satisfy its huge appetite. The tusks are elongated incisors which continue to grow [thr]oughout the elephant's life; these are used extensively in foraging. The ivory is greatly valued and has [bee]n the cause of this animal's dramatic decline throughout Africa over the past two centuries. The large [area]s of the elephant's ears are richly supplied with blood vessels and are essential in helping elephants [cop]e with the intense heat of the African sun.

[T]he African elephant is the largest living land animal. It is also one of the most intelligent and has [a c]omplex social system. Herds of mothers and their offspring range in size from two to twenty four, [and] members of the group rarely move than 50m from their nearest neighbour, keeping contact [thro]ugh low-pitched grumbles and rumbles. The matriarch, recognised as the largest cow, determines [the] activity, direction, and rate of movement. Adolescent male elephants become gradually separated [from] the herd, after which they alternately associate in bachelor herds or wander alone.

The muscular trunk has a variety of functions

Male mass: 5 750kg Shoulder height: 3m
Max. tusk length: 3.4m Max. tusk mass: 100kg
Female mass: 3 800kg Shoulder height: 2.5m
Max. tusk length: 0.75m Max. tusk mass: 30kg
Young: 1 Gestation: 22 months
Longevity: 70 years
Daily food requirement: 160 - 300kg
Daily water requirement: 150 litres

Elephant

Loxodonta africana

A dappled coat provides incredible camouflage

Male mass: 60kg
Total length: 200cm
Shoulder height: 65cm
Female mass: 40kg
Total length: 180cm
Shoulder height: 60cm
Young: 2 - 3
Gestation: 100 days
Longevity: 21 years

Leopard

Panthera pardus

Leopard - The leopard is the living embodiment of stealth, grace and power, and is kilo for kilo perhaps the most powerful of the world's great cats. Its ability to adapt to a wide range of habitat conditions by virtue of its secretive nature and ability to survive on a variety of prey animals (it hunts anything from dung-beetles to antelope twice its weight), make it one of the most successful cats.

Leopards hunt chiefly at night and cover up to 25km of their territory, their excellent hearing and night vision helping them to detect prey. Leopards have incredible patience and may spend hours fastidiously stalking with body low and tense or waiting in ambush until the prey is very close (about three metres) before pouncing on the unsuspecting animal. A leopard often uses its incredible strength to haul its kill up into the branches of a tree. This protects it from scavengers and allows the leopard's meal to last a number of days.

Of the large carnivores, this is the most elusive

Leopards are generally solitary creatures

Leopard's have two to three cubs in a litter

Although frequently seen in trees, leopards spend most of their time on the ground, climbing trees mainly to escape predators or to protect a kill

White rhino having a friendly tussle

A white rhino calf seldom strays far from its mother's side

Rhinoceros - Like horses and tapirs, the rhinoceros' body is supported on three-toed hooves. It differs markedly from these animals though, with its bu

build, its naked or sparsely haired thick hide and the horns on its nose. The horns, extremely varying in size and shape, consist of keratin (like hooves, n

and hair) and are used for protection and as staves in territorial conflicts. They are literally worth their weight in gold, being valued for their use in traditio

Chinese medicine and as material for making dagger handles. Poaching has led to an extreme reduction in their range, and this animal is now found onl

well protected areas.

Two African species, the white and black rhino, and three Asian species survive today. The names of Africa's two rhino species do not refer to t

colouration, both species having grey skin, which may be covered with mud of various hues.

White rhinos are perhaps the largest pure grazers that have ever lived, and can be easily distinguished from the browsing black rhino by their pronounced shoulder hump, far larger size and large, square lips. Black rhino are strictly browsers and use their flexible beak-like upper lip as a grasping tool to select twigs and shoots, which are bitten off with their molars at a characteristic 45 degree angle. They are more inquisitive than the docile white rhino, and if disturbed, move off with their heads held high, their calves following close behind, whereas when white rhino run off, the calves take the lead. Rhinos alternately feed and rest day and night. They are least active during hot weather, when they can be seen sleeping soundly, lying beneath a shady tree or in a mud wallow. Large groups may assemble at wallows, but they are usually seen individually or in small groups. Lone rhino are usually territorial bulls who scent-mark, or non-territorial bulls who live submissively within their territories. Groups commonly consist of a mother and her latest offspring, and occasionally other unrelated juveniles. They may be accompanied for short periods by a territorial bull, which joins long enough to check the cow's reproductive status. Home ranges are dissected by regularly used trails. These are scent-posted with dung middens that are used by both sexes.

A group of black rhino in typical habitat

Black rhino male mass: 1 100kg
shoulder height: 150cm
Female mass: 1 000kg
shoulder height: 140cm
White rhino male mass: 2 100kg
shoulder height: 180cm
Female mass: 1 600kg
shoulder height: 170cm
Top speed: 40kph

Rhinoceros

Black rhino: Diceros bicornis

White rhino: Ceratotherium simum

Black rhino are alert to the warning calls of oxpeckers

Both the male and female buffalo carry horns

Male mass: 750kg
Shoulder height: 160cm
Horn length along curve: 130cm
Female mass: 600kg
Shoulder height: 145cm
Horn length along curve: 60cm
Young: 1
Gestation: 340 days
Life expectancy: 22 years

Buffalo
Syncerus caffer

Buffalo - The large, cattle-like buffalo look extremely placid, swinging their heavily horned heads from side to side as they graze in the cool hours of the day. This impression is far from reality, however: these animals are quick-tempered and savage toward predators and are responsible for the deaths of many people and animals in South Africa each year.

Buffalo have adapted for grazing on coarse grass and are usually found in large mixed herds. The basic units of the herds are stable clans of related cows, which may periodically split away and join up to form larger herds. These 'new' herds are accompanied by adult and sub-adult bulls. Each clan has a dominance hierarchy and its own trusted 'pathfinder' that leads the way to pasture and water.

Buffalo are seasonal breeders, with the dominant bulls mating with all the receptive cows in a clan. The cows each produce a single calf during the summer months. As the calf requires several hours to gain enough strength to follow the herd, the mother and newborn calf are often temporarily left behind and are prone to predation, which is why as few as 20 percent of calves reach maturity.

An oxpecker foraging for troublesome ticks

Bulls have the larger horns and forehead base

As dusk sets in, buffalo forage close to one another. This is the time the herd's principal predator, the lion, starts to prowl

The mother cheetah leaves her cubs at 18 months, whereafter the youngsters form a close sibling group for a further six months

Cheetah - The elegant cheetah, with its characteristic 'tearstains', is the fastest land mammal, reaching speeds of between 95 and 112kph during a chase, which can last up to 300m! They are opportunistic hunters, taking the most abundant and easily captured prey, such as young wildebeest or impala. Their tactic is to rush at their prey after stalking it to within 70 to 100m. The permanently extended claws add traction, while the long, flattened tail acts as both a rudder and a counterweight during the dramatic chase: the cheetah nimbly matches the evasive turns of its victim before knocking it off balance with a timely swipe of its front paw.

The cheetah's agility and speed means that it is less robust than its competitors, however. Because of this, it is easily intimidated into leaving a kill, and it is easily robbed of its prey by lions, leopards, wild dogs, vultures, spotted hyenas and even unassertive brown hyenas. Cheetah try to avoid this competition by hunting predominantly during the day when most other carnivores are inactive and by dragging the kill to cover to avoid being spotted by vultures.

The cheetah's distinctive 'tear-marks'

Male mass: 55kg
Total length: 206cm
Shoulder height: 80cm
Female mass: 45kg
Total length: 190cm
Shoulder height: 75cm
Young: usually 2 - 4
Gestation: 93 days
Life expectancy: 16 years

Cheetah
Acinonynx jubatus

Cheetah often use vantage points to search for prey

Cubs learn to wait undercover while their mothers hunt

13

Zebra calves remain close to their mothers

Male mass: 250kg
Total length: 280cm
Shoulder height: 135cm
Female mass: 230kg
Total length: 290cm
Shoulder height: 130cm
Young: 1, occasionally 2
Gestation: 360 days
Life expectancy: 20 years

Zebra

Burchell's zebra - Equus burchelli

Zebra - Zebras are gregarious animals, living in small, stable family groups known as harems, which consist of a stallion and one or more mares and their foals. Each individual has a different stripe pattern which is thought to serve more to help individuals recognise one another than to help with camouflage. The striping may also confuse lions during a chase and baffle biting flies. The Burchell's zebra is the most common of the three zebra species found in South Africa, and can be recognised by the distinctive greyish 'shadow' between its black stripes. They favour well-watered savanna and are often found together with wildebeest or other antelope, which take advantage of the zebra's keen eyesight as well as its senses of smell and hearing to warn them of danger. Lions and spotted hyenas are their main predators, but the zebra stallion can effectively ward off attack with its aggressive defence and powerful kick.

Young Burchell's zebra mares are released from their natal herd only when the herd stallion has tested the strength of the break-away herd's dominant bachelor stallion over a number of consecutive heat periods. Newcomers to a harem are not welcomed by resident mares and a strict rank hierarchy is enforced when the herd is on the move, drinking and enjoying their favourite pastime: dust-bathing.

A zebra foal being inspected for ticks

Zebra need to drink regularly, as they are adapted to feeding on low-quality grass, which yields little moisture

A female giraffe has thin 'horns', covered in hair

A giraffe's height allows for easy detection of predators

Drinking is an awkward process for a giraffe, and it is the time when they are most vulnerable to attack from predators

Giraffe have only seven vertebrae in their neck

Giraffe - Found only in Africa, south of the Sahara Desert, giraffe fill a niche in the animal kingdom which no other creature can emulate. Their prodigious height, 45cm long prehensile tongue and the modified atlas-axis joint that enables their heads to tilt vertically so that they can feed from the tops of trees which only they can reach. It might be surprising to learn that the giraffe has no more vertebrae in its neck than other mammals - only seven, the same as the squat-necked hippo!

Giraffe are gregarious and are often seen in large scattered herds, which change in composition from day to day. While growing up, males contest for their place in the dominance hierarchy through sometimes violent exchanges of head blows while standing side on and facing opposite directions. The bony growths or 'horns' on the top of the head, serve as clubs during these fights, and the thick black hair covering them tends to be worn away, making it easy to identify males.

Calves weigh about 100kg at birth and can stand within an hour. Despite its stamina, its ability to run at a reasonable speed and the fact that its mother has a strong kick, the giraffe calf has little defence against its principal predator, the lion, and mortality during the first year is high.

Male mass: 1 500kg
Shoulder height: 3m
Top of horns: up to 5.5m
Female mass: 900kg
Shoulder height: 2.5m
Young: 1, rarely 2
Gestation: 475 days
Life expectancy: 28 years

Giraffe
Giraffa camelopardalis

Spotted hyena mass: 65kg

Shoulder height: 85cm

Brown hyena mass: 40kg

Shoulder height: 80cm

Both Spotted & Brown hyena:

Young: 1 - 4

Gestation: 100 days

Life expectancy: 20 years

Wild dog mass: 25kg

Shoulder height: 70cm

Young: 2 - 16

Gestation: 70 days

Life expectancy: 7 years

Hyena & Wild dog

Spotted hyena - Crocuta crocuta

Brown hyena - Hyaena brunnea

Wild dog - Lycaon pictus

Spotted hyenas usually hunt alone

The brown hyena is primarily a scavenger

Spotted hyena - The ungainly spotted hyena is Africa's most abundant large carnivore. Not only are they exceptional scavengers capable of stealing prey from lionesses, they are extremely active and formidable predators, capable of outrunning prey over long distances. They live in large clans, led by the larger, dominant females.

Brown hyena - At around 40kg, the brown hyena is smaller than both the spotted and the rare striped hyena. This shaggy-coated creature is also the shyest of the species, and is not as adept at killing as its spotted cousin. The brown hyena is found only in the arid region of southwest Africa.

Wild dog - Along with the Ethiopian wolf, the wild dog is Africa's most endangered carnivore. Packs are nomadic for most of the year and capture a staggering 85 percent of the animals they chase. Only the dominant pair breeds, and pups are born in a den, and fed and protected by all members of the pack.

The wild dogs' individually patterned, tricoloured coats make them hard to spot when they are resting

The ferocious Nile crocodile, which is effectively a modern day dinosaur, is unusual in that it displays considerable maternal care to both its eggs and hatchlings

Lying almost concealed underwater waiting for prey

Crocodiles cool themselves through their open mouths

Hippos enjoy an active game of wrestling

The cumbersome hippo returns to land at night to feed   *The hippo is the third-largest living land mammal*

Crocodile - Crocodiles are cold-blooded and can often be seen basking on sandbanks to warm emselves up before returning to the water to hunt for fish or to wait in ambush for animals that come drink. They are incredibly stealthy and cunning, and they use their long, powerful tails to launch emselves out of the water at incredible speed to grab animals the size of wildebeest, which are then owned underwater. While crocodiles are feared throughout the African continent as man-eaters, it is e hippo that accounts for more deaths in Africa each year.

Hippopotamus - Hippos are often seen in the company of crocodiles during the day, when they st in the water to protect their bare, sensitive skin from the sun's harmful rays. At night hippos leave the ater to forage on land, and they return shortly before dawn, which is when most of the fatal encounters th Man occur. Female hippos give birth to a single calf in a secluded section of shallow water. The calf able to swim within a few minutes of birth and is able to suckle underwater.

Crocodile mass: up to 1 000kg
Length: up to 6m
Clutch size: 90 eggs
Gestation: 4 months
Sex of hatchlings determined by
average sand temperature
Can remain underwater for one hour
Hippopotamus mass: 15 000kg
shoulder height: 150cm
Life expectancy: 40 years
Young: 1, rarely 2
Gestation: 240 days
Can remain underwater for 6 minutes

Crocodile & Hippopotamus

Crocodile - *Crocodylus niloticus*

Hippo - *Hippopotamus amphibious*

Only the male impala grow horns

Impala mass: 50kg Shoulder height: 90cm
Horns: 80cm (males only)
Springbok mass: 40kg Shoulder height: 75cm
Horns: 45cm (both sexes)
Gemsbok mass: 220kg Shoulder height: 120cm
Horns: 110cm (both sexes)

Antelope

Impala - Aepyceros melampus
Springbok - Antidorcas marsupialis
Gemsbok - Oryx gazella

The majority and widest variety of antelopes on Earth occur on the African continent, and 37 of the occur in South Africa.

Impala - The graceful and agile impala is by far the most common antelope on the savann. This animal has a distinct marking on the rump, resembling the arches of the MacDonald's logo ar somewhat ironically, they are the favoured fast food of most predators! Despite their high predation, th are very successful, due largely to their high birth rate and ability to maintain good condition long into dry season. They achieve this by switching their feeding from grass to more nutritious browse.

Springbok - Until 1896, the endemic springbok would migrate southwards in times of droug covering the landscape in herds many thousands strong. Springbok are famous for their 'pronking repeated stiff-legged bounces high into the air. This peculiar behaviour is usually performed in respor to the sighting of a predator, and is thought to function as a warning to the rest of the herd and to indic to the predator that it is fit enough to fight.

Gemsbok - The gemsbok often roams the same arid habitats as the springbok, but is also able survive in the dunes of the Namib Desert. The impressive rapier-shaped horns are used by males wh sparring for dominance and also to ward off predators such as spotted hyena and lion.

Female impala live together in breeding herds

Springbok use moisture from plants to thrive in arid areas

Male and female gemsbok sport rapier-shaped horns

In late summer adult impala rams leave bachelor herds to establish small territories for the three-week long rut

A handsome male kudu shows off his spiral horns

As the largest antelope, adult Eland are preyed upon only by lions and spotted hyena

The wildebeest roams the open veld in herds of up to fifty

Kudu - The kudu is one of Africa's greatest showpieces, the males' spiral-shaped horns reaching to 1.8m in length. Like their closest relative, the nyala, they also have white spots and chevrons on the face, with white stripes on the flanks, which vary in number, spacing and pattern.

Eland - This commanding-looking animal is the world's largest antelope, males growing up to a shoulder height of 1.7m and weighing approximately 900kg. However, despite its large physique, the eland is a remarkably agile antelope, able to leap over regular-sized fencing. Their fawn-coloured coats carry the distinctive vertical white stripes, and both males and females have thick, tightly spiralled horns. The eland is a browser, dieting on a wide variety of plant species, and eating even the fruit of tsamas and gemsbok cucumbers if water is scarce. The eland herd is very protective of its young, and when threatened by predators, the herd forms a front, with the largest males in the lead and the females and calves protected behind them.

Wildebeest - The bearded wildebeest are often referred to as 'Clowns of the Veld' due to their amusing antics and characteristic head and tail tossing. They are exceptionally well built with particularly massive shoulders, making them swift runners. The more common blue wildebeest has outward sweeping horns, while the lighter black wildebeest has frontward-sweeping horns and a white tail. Blue wildebeest have one of the most closely synchronised births of all antelope, with 80 to 90 percent of the calves being born within three weeks. The calves can stand within three to five minutes of birth and run with the mother immediately thereafter.

The striking kudu sports distinctive stripes

Kudu mass: 200kg Shoulder height: 145cm
Horns: 160cm (both sexes)
Eland mass: 900kg Shoulder height: 1.7m
Horns: 75cm (both sexes)
Blue wildebeest mass: 230kg Shoulder height: 130cm
Black wildebeest mass: 140kg Shoulder height: 115cm
Life expectancy: 18 years Young: 1, rarely 2
Gestation: 250 days

Kudu - Tragelaphus strepsiceros
Eland - Taurotragus oryx
Blue wildebeest - Connochaetes taurinus
Black wildebeest - Connochaetes gnou

Black-backed jackal mass: 8kg

Life expectancy: 10 years

Young: 2 - 10

Side-striped jackal mass: 9kg

Life expectancy: 11 years

Young: 1 - 4

Bat-eared fox mass: 4kg

Life expectancy: 5.5 years

Young: 2 - 6

Cape fox mass: 3kg

Young: 3 - 5

Jackals & Foxes

Black-backed jackal - *Canis mesomelas*

Side-striped jackal - *Canis adastus*

Bat-eared fox - *Otocyon megalotis*

Cape fox - *Vulpes chama*

Black-backed jackals are diurnal, but also hunt at night

Bat-eared fox pups stay close to the safety of their de

Jackals - A white tail tip distinguishes the side-striped jackal from the more common and mor distinctively marked black-backed jackal. Both jackal species have an amazing ability to find food, ar although the black-backed jackal is a more accomplished scavenger while the side-striped jackal predominantly a fruit eater, both species also actively hunt for small mammals, reptiles and invertebrate Jackals breed in abandoned holes, and both parents return at 2 to 3 hourly intervals through the night t feed weaned pups with food carried back in the mouth or regurgitated. Of the pups that survive the firs six months, one or two remain in the parent's territory to assist in rearing young.

Foxes - Bat-eared foxes have remarkably large ears, which are used like twin-dish antennae to pic up and pinpoint the faint stirrings of insects such as dung beetle larvae buried 15 to 30cm undergroun or their principal prey, the harvester termite. The beautiful and dainty Cape fox is one of the smalles embers of the dog family. It is South Africa's only true fox and is a strictly nocturnal predator, preying on mice, insects, and other small animals. Both species e usually seen in pairs and give birth to litters in underground dens in late spring. They are extremely agile predators which are hard to catch, having the ability zig-zag and change course while running at speed.

The small Cape fox is one of the few carnivores endemic to South Africa

Anteaters excavate their homes from termitaria

Anteater mass: 50kg Shoulder height: 60cm
Life expectancy: 18 years
Young: 1, rarely 2 Gestation: 7 months
Pangolin mass: 16kg Length: 80cm
Life expectancy: 12 years
Young: 1, rarely 2 Gestation: 5 months
Young carried on back

Anteater & Pangolin

Anteater - Orycteropus afer

Pangolin - Cercopithecus albogularis

Anteater and Pangolin - The curious-looking antbear and pangolin are both adapted to hunt and capture the same aggressive insects – termites and ants – using their long noses to sniff them out, the long, curved front claws to dig them out from beneath the soil, and their long, sticky tongues to lap them up. Being predominantly nocturnal, they face the danger of bumping into prowling predators such as lions and hyenas. While the antbear runs for the nearest burrow when threatened, the lumbering pangolin rolls up into a tight ball and relies on its covering of overlapping scales for protection.

Pangolins walk on their hind legs, using their tails to balance

Warthog and Bushpig - Warthogs are perhaps best known for their habit of running away from danger with their tails extended aerial-like into the air and their curious facial warts. Another distinguishing mark of the warthog is its tusks, of which the boars have two pairs and the smaller sows one. The warthog's hairier relative, the bushpig, is nocturnal and less well known, but has an equally sharp set of canine tusks. These make it a formidable adversary, to which many an indignant leopard would testify.

Although both warthogs and bushpigs are gregarious, living in family groups known as 'sounders', they differ greatly in their social organisation and behaviour. While a bushpig boar leads and protects his family, warthog boars are promiscuous and mingle only to check for sows in oestrus, having little to do with the social life of the group.

At night bushpigs forage, while warthogs lie together in one of up to ten secure, often disused

This stocky bush pig has razor-sharp lower tusks

antbear holes within their home range. These holes are very important in the life of the warthog, affording protection against sun, bad weather and predators. Warthogs give birth to their hairless young within a raised recess of the hole, while bushpigs gather a nest of grass up to one metre high to form a refuge into which they burrow and give birth.

A warthog sow is very watchful over her vulnerable litter

Warthog mass: 70kg Shoulder height: 65cm
Life expectancy: 18 years
Young: 2 - 8 Gestation: 165 days
Bushpig mass: 60kg Shoulder height: 65cm
Life expectancy: 13 years
Young: 3 - 8 Gestation: 125 days

Warthog & Bushpig

Warthog - _Phacochoerus aethiopicus_

Bushpig - _Potamochoerus porcus_

An African wild cat sleeping in the fork of a tree

The serval's large ears can pinpoint faint sounds

Small-spotted genets emerge at dusk to hunt

African wild cat - The African wild cat is the ancestor of the domestic cat, having been domesticated in Egypt about 6 000 years ago to keep rats and mice out of granaries. Today the integrity of the species is threatened by in-breeding with domestic cats which have been introduced wherever people have settled. Although it is the most common and widespread of Africa's cats, it is little known but, like the domestic cat, it is a nocturnal hunter, preying mostly on mice and rats.

Serval - Like most cats, the unobtrusive serval is nocturnal and solitary, but it is one of the few that favour wetland areas. Here it hunts rodents, especially vlei rats, which it catches by pouncing from up to 4m away.

Small-spotted genet - The nocturnal small-spotted genets are as much at home on the ground as they are in trees, but they take refuge when threatened by larger predators. Under stress they release a strong, musky odour from their scent glands, which may help deter predators, but is usually used for marking territories and conveying information about breeding status.

Caracal - A sighting of a caracal in the wild is a special treat, as they are well camouflaged and very secretive. Caracal are mainly nocturnal and are very seldom seen during the day. They often use their very strong hind limbs to launch themselves high into the air to catch birds in flight.

Surricate - Being a small carnivore, little bigger than the tassel of a lion's tail, surricates face the dual problem of being both predator and prey. They overcome threat by living in tight-knit groups which show a great degree of co-operation. They are thus able to dig for lizards and beetle grubs while keeping a look-out for birds of prey, with each individual taking a turn to act as a sentinel while the pack is foraging. Burrows which are usually appropriated from ground squirrels, are used as a refuge when the surricates are threatened. These are extensive, have many entrances and stretch as deep as two metres underground.

Mongoose - Banded mongooses also live in cohesive packs. The females have synchronised births and then care for their young communally. If threatened by a predator up to the size of a jackal, mongooses may put up a collective defence by bunching tightly and advancing, bristling and growling, towards it. Insects are their main food source, but the contents of eggs also provide them with a good source of nutrition. To break open an egg, the mongoose ingeniously uses its front legs to hurl the egg between its rear legs onto a stone.

Caracals have a characteristic tuft of black hair on their ears

Surricates soaking up the morning sun

African wild cat mass: 4.5kg
Length: 85cm Life expectancy: 23 years
Young: 2 - 3
Serval mass: 12kg Length: 110cm
Life expectancy: 17 years
Young: 1 - 6
Small-spotted genet mass: 2kg
Length: 95cm Life expectancy: 14 years
Young: 1 - 4
Caracal mass: 12kg
Length: 110cm Life expectancy: 17 years
Young: 1 - 6
Surricate mass: 0.7kg Length: 50cm
Life expectancy: 10 years

Small Carnivores

African wild cat - *Felis lybica*
Serval - *Filis serval*
Small-spotted genet - *Genetta genetta*
Caracal - *Felis caracal*
Surricate - *Suricata suricatta*

Chacma baboons are omnivorous, but prefer fruit

Vervet monkey mass: 5kg Length: 1.1m
Life expectancy: 12 years
Young: 1, rarely 2 Gestation: 200 days
Chacma baboon mass: 25kg Length: 1.4m
Life expectancy: 18 years
Young: 1, rarely 2 Gestation: 187 days

Primates

Vervet monkey - Cercopithecus aethiops
Chacma baboon - Papio cynocephalus
ursinus

Primates - The chacma baboon and vervet monkey are South Africa's most abundant and widespread primates and can provide hours of entertaining viewing. They are both diurnal and gregarious and occur in large troops with complex social hierarchies whose members sleep, forage and rest together, and who jointly defend the home range. Females form the core of the troop and remain in the troop of their birth throughout their lives, while males migrate as adolescents to join other troops as lower ranking males. The troops consist of a number of families known as 'kinship groups' accompanied by several large, high-ranking males who share in the troop's offensive and defensive actions. Troops have distinct dominance hierarchies and are not simply one big happy family as they may initially appear. Dominance is established through fighting, and it is maintained through threatening eyelid displays and displays of their dental weaponry.

Being omnivores with a predominantly vegetarian diet, vervet monkeys and chacma baboons have teeth very similar to those of humans. Their diets also overlap considerably, but the larger baboons feed additionally on birds' eggs and even lizards, young vervet monkeys and new-born antelope when they can catch them. The monkeys and baboons often forage in the same food trees, but the larger baboons are always dominant, except on the smallest outer branches.